Landscaping for Wildlife
By Jen Karetnick

Landscaping for Wildlife
©2012, Jen Karetnick
ISBN: 978-1-937806-03-3
Big Wonderful Press, LLC
Brooklyn, NY

Cover Photograph by Jaime Ferreyros
All Rights Reserved.

Acknowledgments

Carpe Articulum, "Landscaping for Wildlife"
The Drexel Online Journal, "Only Swan"
Extracts, "Gulf," "Interview with My Son before Snorkeling," "Love Poem for the Purple Gallinule"
Folly, "Echolalia"
Isotope, "Adult Congregate Living Facility"
jerseyworks, "On Lion Road"
Journal of New Jersey Poets, "After Not Jogging for Three Months, Green Township, New Jersey"
OCHO, "Bush Walk Terzanelle"
Paper Salad Poetry Journal, "Fall"
Pearl, "Crossing the Blood/Brain Barrier"
The Pinehurst Journal, "A Gesture"
Radius, "American Dog Terrorists"
Southern Arts Journal, "To a Girl Glimpsed from a Country Road"
Temenos, "Green Iguana Freeze"
Virtual Word, "Jersey Corn"

POEMS

Adult Congregate Living Facility 5
Echolalia 6
Shrimp Baby Sestina 7
Only Swan 9
Love Poem for the Purple Gallinule 10
For a Lazy Provider, Or; To a Cat Toying with a Snake 11
Canoe Tripping 12
Bush Walk Terzanelle 13
Interview with My Son before Snorkeling 14
The Strength of Conch 15
Gulf 17
The Sound of Global Warming: 18
Brief Renku with Myself 18
Green Iguana Freeze 19
Landscaping for Wildlife 22
Sevenling: Dachshund Winterfest 23
A Gesture 24
Microclimates 25
Sweat Equity 26
Garden Poem 27
Recycling 28
To a Girl Glimpsed from a Country Road 29
Jersey Corn 30
On Orchestras and Falconry 31
New England Music Camp 32
Sustain 33
On Hand-Tying a Tussie-Mussie 34
After Not Jogging for Three Months, ... 35
Green Township, New Jersey 35
Crossing the Blood/Brain Barrier 36
Fall 37
American Dog Terrorists 38
The Danger of Self-Analysis 39
On Lion Road 40

Adult Congregate Living Facility

Peacocks nest on the roof of Nightingale Manor.
Beneath them, the inmates practice their manners—

the screamer, the barker, the wheel-chaired tree hugger
who rolls mechanically to all manner

of reachable trunks. The barker woofs at whoever's
near, his yips and growls merely a manner

of speaking; the neighborhood dogs clear
fences to find one soul so canine-mannered,

gathering, it sounds like, at my house next door.
The screamer roars prayers with the mannered

consistency of a gas lawn-mower,
despite the aides' reminders to mind his manners,

and I shout, too, to any god there is for a measure
of silence to pervade my own echoing manor,

until the peacocks reproach me with tail-feathers
housebroken as wood, from what I can see of their manner.

Echolalia

Outside, the incessant wails of peacocks,
Clever mimics of my baby's colic
Rising and rising in the humid night,
Propel me from my temporal seat.
Back arching, her legs point into pitchforks,
Stabbing my ribs as we rock and walk.
The doctor says don't over-stimulate,
Try not to bore her, burp more, medicate.
Startled, her tongue fans out to explore
Her mouth, clownish, stained with cherry-flavor
Tylenol, Orajel, Mylicon, wine
—whatever liquid works to keep me calm—
Placebos until she wears herself out.
Only she knows what this is all about.

Only she knows what this is all about:
Placebos until she wears herself out,
Whatever liquid works to keep me calm
—Tylenol, Orajel, Mylicon, wine—
Her mouth clownish, stained with cherry flavor.
Startled, her tongue fans out to explore.
Try not to bore her, burp more, medicate.
The doctor says don't over-stimulate.
Stabbing my ribs as we rock and walk,
Back arching, her legs point into pitchforks,
Propel me from my temporal seat.
Rising and rising in the humid night,
Clever mimics of my baby's colic,
Outside, the incessant wails of peacocks.

Shrimp Baby Sestina
*from "Shrimp Boat Captain Delivers Baby at Sea,"
AP newswire, August 30, 2007*

With the ragged black batwings of nets
ready to splay wide and swing close
over a receiving blanket of ice in crates,
and a skeleton three-person crew,
the boat dove into the Florida ocean
in search of wild American shrimp.

Few storms were predicted to disturb the shrimp
that year, and the industry stood to net
gains, or at least recoup the lost ocean
sunsets, unheard birdcalls and beers still closed
in the cans from previous seasons when crews
were living on shore, boatless, out of crates.

The boat itself seemed made out of crates
too rickety to hold stock as harmless as shrimp,
and an equally unbalanced crew.
Still, the woman wasn't due yet, and the net
of her belly should have kept the baby close
in his climate-controlled, private ocean.

Even a shrimp knows never to trust an ocean,
though, not completely, no matter how warm. Crates
that are traps lie in wait, ready to close.
And small, curved, pink, this particular shrimp
obeyed the instinct to escape the net,
breaking through placental barriers, a crew

of one on his first journey. The crew
responded the way any would, boiling ocean
water, sterilizing the twine from nets
and making a pallet on top of crates.
But dangling feet first, the shrimp got caught,
strangling, the captain recalled, too close

to birth. So he waited for a wave to close
and open her, slipped a hand in to crew
him home and tied off the cord into a shrimp,
though he'd never before sailed this ocean.
After, he unloaded the family with the crates,
posed for the paper in front of his nets,

held the baby close and then looked to the ocean;
diminished, the crew set out with its crates,
the boat sighing for lack of shrimp in its nets.

Only Swan

Waggling wing-feathers like a tongue,
the male urges his solitary clan
away from Taylor Lake, mud-puddle manned
by Canadian geese and their terrible young
who shit, on average, twenty-eight times
a day. On the other shore, great blue heron
honk, blaring as traffic. The swans have gone
walk-about before with clipped limbs, mimes
to ridicule once out of the slime, but the man
who maintains the weeds of near fields herds
back the family, watering the single,
pampered signet. He fears for the dandelions
webbing paved gravel. Mothered and fathered
by lovers, this swan won't be raised to mingle.

Love Poem for the Purple Gallinule

From ficus to sawgrass, spatterdock to mangrove,
with the fidgety gravity of a balloon losing helium,
the purple gallinule skips over the skin of the glades,
freckle to sunspot like the sheen on the surface of oil

upon water. His mate is somewhere nearby. Or is it
her mate? Rare for birds, both sexes preen—each other
a reflection, purple into green, double gait feathering
from ficus to sawgrass, spatterdock to mangrove—

and both parent the clutch of eggs floating in a bowl
of grasses and tree stems on a tussock or in a thicket,
the free-roaming bird bearing gifts for the babysitter
with the fidgety gravity of a balloon losing helium,

bringing home a frog or dragonfly. Always, this swamp
hen drops a leaf in the nest before trading duties,
to be used for the expansion of roof and a ramp.
The purple gallinule skips over the skin of the glades,

stalking the lily pads with clown feet, reluctant in flight
but canonical in canals. He takes only one mate for life,
and should one die, the other will, too, become no more than
a freckle or sunspot like the sheen on the surface of oil.

For a Lazy Provider, Or; To a Cat Toying with a Snake

There is no poison in its open mouth,
its rubbery length (double yours), its futile
tail; and still, there is little that is uncouth
about your game, no teeth or claws of ill
will, no intent beyond a tease. I've seen
you and your grey tabby siblings in haste,
your mom raiding my garbage for the cans
of tunafish, empty but for dried paste;
I noticed you pinned under the one-eyed
black-and-white tom over there in the grass;
and as you poke and prod but don't move to eat
I watch now with my kids from behind glass.
Calling you feral is an oversight.
You're nothing but a well-fed suburbanite.

Canoe Tripping
    --in Jonathan Dickinson State Park, Florida

The crisp of baked clay, still as a clock face,
the fourteen-foot bull gator hunted, we heard,
just around the bend, under the shirred
ruffs of air plants clinging to the cases
of eucalyptus trees, near rumored Swamp Apes.
The bullet we stroked seemed the length
of his leather but inferior in strength,
the shellacked hull hollow. We paddled to gape
but gleaned only his leftover aplenty,
the shape of where he'd been a stillness
in the eddies – but sure, we'd seen him, we told
other floaters, a big 'un at eighteen feet, twenty,
in the river where it runs wide as Loch Ness
and fresh as the Fountain of Youth, whirlpooled.

Bush Walk Terzanelle
--for Matthew Harding, Singita Head Guide

The rules on how to meet big game on foot,
should the knob thorn be parted by a trunk
as in the dried-up riverbed you root

for shells and linger behind the last gun,
are written in a font that plays on mute:
Should the knob thorn be parted by a trunk,

take a stand. Stand still. If you run, you're food
for the croc whose tail couldn't be more frank,
his trail written in a font that plays on mute;

for the lions, marked by blood, age and rank;
for the hyena who leaves her bony soot.
The croc whose tail couldn't be more frank

the ranger who would protect you like loot
might be able to hit in the shank,
but consider the damage mutual.

So take them as gospel or get a boot
directed toward a khaki-covered shank—
these rules on how to meet big game on foot
as in the dried-up riverbed you root.

Interview with My Son before Snorkeling
--at *The Lodge at Kurá Hulanda, Curaçao*

"Is there anything dangerous here?" he asked,
waddling backwards, flippers flapping as he crossed

the equator between stones and sand into surf, fresh off
a week of survivors' stories of sneak-attack tigers

and great whites breaching the Discovery Channel.
("I didn't even know I was in a shark until I opened

my eyes and saw teeth, and he started thrashing
me about," related the tank-less abalone diver

from New Zealand, "because that's what sharks do.
That's when I felt fear.") "No," I lied, "there's nothing,"

though I am from the *Jaws* generation and see a dorsal
tipping every wave, about to saw through my string bikini.

I tightened my son's mask so it would mark him like sleep,
showed him how to bite down on the mouthpiece

the way a dog clenches his toy. Nothing about breathing
underwater is comfortable, nor should it be.

For brief seconds on his own he collected brain coral,
observed eels scooting under rocks, and I wondered

as all mothers wonder if this is the one I'll be allowed
to keep, before he finned up from behind to slip into mine

his growing, shriveled hand, that once-familiar
fish swimming in the oceanic eddies of my body.

The Strength of Conch
    -- *off the coast of Belize*

They make no resistance when you pluck them
from the ocean floor; they don't bite or struggle
or spray urine, poison, ink. Their spiky crowns alone

might deter a predator in need of dental work
but not one as hungry and experimental
as a human, who recognizes no boundaries—

not climates non-conducive to supporting life
without assistance, not the caste regulations
observed meticulously by most of the rest

of the food chain. But put them in a bucket
with no seawater to keep them moist
and when you have turned your attention

to your freshly uncapped Belikan premium,
allowing the trolling lines to go on catching nothing
by themselves, they will reach out a single foot,

callused as those that trudge the dusty tracks
from Placencia Beach to Seine Bight several times a day,
and push and rock to their release, hoping the splash

as they re-enter familiar territory will be mistaken
for that of a tern inquiring about the catch of the day.
Don't be fooled. Once again on the sea bed,

maybe twelve feet under, they are as caught as sand.
This time, don't delay. Hammer a spike
just under the pink-stained ruff and grab the belly

with your hand angled just so. Then harvest the "strength,"
a clear tube of salty gelatin no bigger than a baby eel.
An aphrodisiac, the Belizeans claim, which does you little good

if you're traveling alone. No matter. The fishermen delight
in watching a woman down the slippery string,
and like the conch meat itself, surprisingly small

once cleaned, and which must be pounded
to a certain level of tenderness before lip-smacking
consumption, in the end it's hardly worth the fuss.

Gulf

The edge of the Atlantic froths like the milk
she blows bubbles into through a straw
in her glass even when *Papí* says, "*No, gordita,*"
eyelet through which she pokes her pinky fingers,
irresistible lace like the trim on the skirt
of her bathing suit, yellow as her dreams
and the only one she will wear no matter
how many times *Mamí* pulls from her drawer
the bikini with the terrifying flowers. It is the hour
when all creatures that could pinch her toes
nest in the hot pillows of sand they call home,
but not yet time for the sandwich that will hold
her fingerprints like Play-Doh or the papaya, grainy
with bees. Her shadow, that unrelenting sister,
reflects only her puff of hair, squat and clownish.
She is not allowed to swim today. There is oil
in the water, *Mamí* says, and tar balls bobbing
just below the surface like jellyfish. She rubs
her thighs, slick with sunscreen, and wonders
how many children must have jumped into this
water before they were supposed to, before
the smell of coconut had seeped into their skin,
to have caused such a stain that she now must
stand under this sun, sweating, and be punished.

**The Sound of Global Warming:
Brief Renku with Myself**

I.
Traffic rushes by
Like one thousand rivers fed
By icecaps melting.

II.
All night, iguanas
Thud to the ground like mangos.
Inside, they're awake.

Green Iguana Freeze
from a fragment of Sappho

I.

"Sweetbitter unmanageable
creature who steals" in to my pool,

eats your share of fruit and then some,
dive into this promised freedom

from live oak branch or the deck rail,
unripe to the tip of your tail.

Non-native, also not welcome,
dive into this promised freedom

offered by lackadaisical
predators, where plenty can fill

your hollow, prehistoric drum.
Dive into this promised freedom

though you will leave it behind foul
with your fibrous mango stool,

and chew a hole through my mesh frame.
Dive into this promised freedom

while the weather lasts, while
the pythons in the swamp still rule,

testing my love of the kingdom.
Dive into this promised freedom

and when the wind turns to a chill
that portends cold-blooded hell,

I'll fan the flames to keep warm
your stiff-legged dive to freedom.

II.

"Sweetbitter unmanageable
creature who steals" in to my pool,

eats your share of fruit and then some,
you test my love of the kingdom.

From live oak branch or the deck rail,
unripe to the tip of your tail—

non-native, also not welcome—
dive into this promised freedom

offered by lackadaisical
predators, where plenty can fill

the hollow, prehistoric drum
testing my love of the kingdom,

though you will leave it behind foul
with your fibrous mango stool,

and chew a hole through my mesh frame.
Dive into this promised freedom

while the weather lasts, while
the pythons in the swamp still rule

and 'gators have not yet gone numb.
You have no place in my kingdom,

but when the wind turns to a chill
that portends cold-blooded hell,

I'll fan the flames to keep warm
your stiff-legged dive to freedom.

Landscaping for Wildlife

First, fire the gardener, then disable the gas-powered mower.
Open yourself to the crabgrass creeping over flagstone
patios with the abandon of mold, along with the weeds

and avocado seedlings that take root from pits; welcome
a collection of cloudbursts seeping in under the door
of the garage every so often from the natural pool you built

from a kit that cost $99.99 at the K-Mart Garden Center;
embrace the mold itself. Think about planting vertically.
Provide ground cover, a food source. Remove everything

non-native, including yourself. It's only natural that the dead
coconut palms, lopped off halfway and left standing, should
house the red-bellied woodpeckers that killed them to begin with

and that the orchard, polluted by possum shit, be a nightclub
for rodents who fight over the flesh of lychee and carambola,
leaving fruit half-eaten, brown with rot and bug-blown.

Should you desire the tin-roof company of Caribbean parrots,
or wish to lure the fox and her future kits to den under your deck,
this is only the beginning of the compost you will have to dwell on.

Sevenling: Dachshund Winterfest

"Dang, these dogs are mighty popular down here,"
a tourist, eyes leashed to that brindle, this piebald,
those matching double dapples, comments on
     South Beach.

I hum him the tune to the Dach Song, drag my own
smooth chocolate specimen, naked among the tutus,
the hot dog buns, the motorcycle vests, away from
     the gathering.

The greetings are effusive, but the leave-takings go
     unnoticed.

A Gesture

Repeated as we walked,
our hands sifting air,
a school of bottlenose
gifted us with their play,
dousing the pier,
carving the waves.
Sunset's swift mantilla
had purpled the sky,
and impressed by the rare oil
of glistening fins and clouds,
light striking on every surface,
his fingers grazed mine,
withdrew, then came shyly to rest.
Loss was only our first imagining.

Microclimates

Take this graft of mango,
this rooting carambola.

Plant them south,
away from my gaze,

filled and filling again
with thumping fruit.

In front of you may be
bridges built like a marathon,

but land will find you
on the other side,

and though the water
lingers tart as limes,

there is plenty to sustain
these cuttings on the way.

Sweat Equity

The heat is green and I will earn it
under the Choquette avocado trees
with the juice of grass on the shovel bit
and the first decapitations of weeds.

Under the Choquette avocado trees
is the worst place to plant any garden,
where the first decapitations of weeds
is just one key on the ring of the warden.

It's the worst place to plant any garden
where the competition of roots is grave,
just one key on the ring of the warden,
unlocking the seeds of what not to save.

Where the competition of roots is grave,
with the juice of grass on the shovel bit
unlocking the seeds of what not to save,
the heat is green and I will earn it.

Garden Poem

What do potato beds need?
Long digs. Deep holes. Real toil.

What have tomato vines decreed?
At dawn and dusk, floodwater.

What do carrots require?
Pockets to push through soil.

What do banana trees wish for?
A well-bred work force: Daughters.

Recycling

"It's not the week for commingling," she said,
"only paper," washing out cans of black beans

at the sink and jars of marinated beets,
earth and the blood of roots funneling down

the drain in a stream almost bilingual,
then stacking them in the rack to steam

and wait for their time like grapes,
dropped and poised for the crush. Outside,

the deer, proliferated in triplicate,
hid from the hunters who swept the skies,

bird shot bracketing the day
as it turned from wing-tucked sleep

and then again as it moved into the shortest
of shadows, each rifle crack a dried bean

rattling around in a tin can, unreconstituted,
each trophy wrapped in the paper of the season.

To a Girl Glimpsed from a Country Road

What a long walk to play
with the kid next door—

from farmhouse to Federal
or Moravian to Victorian

or ranch to cotton-hued Colonial
on feet that, shortened to the Morgan,

counter-cantered the dusty edge
of the show ring at the Warren County Fair

or the Sussex, preferable for the size
of its forty-thousand-dollar purse

—and in this heat, too, an index
upward of ninety-three degrees

evidenced by the Delaware dishwater
piled up in drought-polished patches,

stones a slush of crushed ice
or bridges quick as minutes

when viewed from the side
of another state—the storm

galloping up just might beat you
to the border of hay bales

and wraparound porches, corn
stalks kneeling as you trot past

slower than you like but certain
always of direction as a judge—

Jersey Corn

The city starts with the strains
of June's brick-lightening dawn.
All over town, loud lamps go off duty,
toning down one by one.

East side. Stands of Jersey corn
planted in a median's
compost of cans, piss, and rain-pocked cement
take the melodies on,

rustling silk, leaves—the sweet
hopeful strings of a quartet
hired to point the guests dancing to brass
toward a more modest exit.

On Orchestras and Falconry

He conducts like a lawyer, accusing at first draw,
pleading next with the rows of cellists
who watch with one great eye
his case pressed against the violinists.

He conducts, gyrfalcon on the wing
of a leathered arm, booted in his mossy salon,
engaged to the hunt, ears pricked to the song
of the bells attached to outstretched talons.

He conducts, taut on the soles of his feet as his baton
draws Picassos, delineates Fibonacci theories,
makes periodic tables based on the beats of drums,
composes recipes hot with the bite of electricity.

He conducts, fingers syncopating on the hand
holding the traces of the feathered soloist,
at his back the forest's breath like the wind
blowing glissandos up the slide of the trombonist.

Oh pheasants, beware, and clarinetists quivering
in the thicket of strings. He can sweep the sky
free of blue. He conducts. Ask yourself how long
you can hide. Ask yourself what you must pay.

New England Music Camp

Sunshine's noon sizzle,
the fervent haying of grass.
Beetles buzz, tumble

around the flagpole's
lackadaisical shadow.
Hummingbirds treble.

In the sticky sap,
the glacial lake's mercury
licks at rocky lips.

The groove underscored,
released by an hour's taut
and stretch, the choir

eclipses this song—
what summer has always sung.
I breathe in and change.

Sustain
    --for Gundlach Bundschu

A melody can take care of itself.
But a finish requires concentration.
Reduce those bright notes with a dose of bass clef.
Soften harsh tannins with an oaky oration.

A finish requires intense concentration,
like the harvest dripping from its vinous shelf.
Soften harsh tannins with an oaky oration,
one that addresses its audiences by whole, not half.

Like the harvest hanging from its vinous shelf,
the soil seeks from us a natural conclusion,
one addressing its audience by whole, not half,
for this vintage and the winery's duration.

The earth asks only for a natural conclusion:
Reduce those bright notes with a dose of bass clef—
not just for one vintage but for the duration—
and the melody forever will take care of itself.

On Hand-Tying a Tussie-Mussie
    -- from a lesson given by my sister

Cross the stems to get a larger bouquet;
add color and turn to hold upright.
In every supermarket and every color known to man,
you can always find an alstromeria to match your outfit.

Add color and turn to hold upright.
Some flowers need more water, some need less.
You can always find an alstromeria to match your outfit.
Cut roses underwater and at an angle so they can drink.

Some flowers need more water, some need less.
Make it into a metaphor, or a substitution.
Cut roses underwater and at an angle so they can drink.
It's more like nature to have buds that aren't open.

Make it into a metaphor, or a substitution.
Cross the stems to get a larger bouquet.
It's more like nature to have buds that aren't open,
in every supermarket and every color known to man.

After Not Jogging for Three Months, Green Township, New Jersey

> *Walk with yourself*
> *to be with your selves...*
>   -- Yolanda Pantin

The pull begins deep
in the muscles the way
acid takes root in the teeth.

Stallions show me their
saffron tools as blinkered,
they trot and buck.

A caravan of Harleys
bank down the hill
I run up, most of them red

as my face, I imagine;
I can't tell if the riders
wave to me or each other

or empty flower beds,
combed like graves
for bulbs yet to be born.

A hawk paces me. I glimpse
his hunt through maples
naked as summer creeks,

lapping the stubbed cornfields.
Cold spring. Tomorrow
will bring a strain, the rub.

Crossing the Blood/Brain Barrier

     The bee blew in through the box on the wall, old box that in June breathed bees, honeycombed with coils that didn't cool. "Gotta fix that damn box," Dad said. Though he wasn't home when Yellow Jacket buzzed the tops of our pigtails, its fat body between wings like an apple clasped between hands.
     We abandoned hands of war in mid-discard and ran to Grandma Bea, babysitter allergic to the hypodermic sting but with ideas like bees—thoughts of pitting kings against queens, and twos against threes. She left off stirring the macaroni-and-cheese to thrust Good Housekeeping until the rolled edges caught it midsection... Yellow Jacket's astonished carcass curling in muted sunlight as the magazine twitched back to flat, and her arm back to her spoon...
     Years later that same right arm twitching, palsied, a folded wing. A queen under siege can't recall her subjects so I fly back to her but I'm late, and the brittle walls I settle into smell of smoke, coated with the gold of an advancing flame...

Fall

Tickling the roof
tiles, rain, once again,
the heavy master of gravity

drawing it down to the last
undestroyed canefields,
the last surviving limes. Acorns,

acorns of light
drops announce the autumn
to these days

as if the earth
hadn't already anointed harvest
with regret.

American Dog Terrorists

Blood is what they want so it's blood
they'll get. Crawling from shrubs they'll
sabotage the host, sabotage
being their first nature, being
not animals, not humans, not
insects but spiders, ticks in sects,
eggs carried like ideas, eggs
the seeds of disease, unnoticed the
way they attach, feed, make headway
in reorganizing origin.

The Danger of Self-Analysis

A different world cannot be built
by indifferent people. This is how shame is built.

And guilt. And charity auctions to provide
relief, the salve. We are with fault lines, built

like the crust of the earth, plates filled with flaws
rubbing against each other at a table built

too small for the company it keeps. I see I am
a volcano, cracked and bleeding, built

fertile enough to grow greens on my slopes
but always a smoky worry, the built-

up threat of a head of steam. So I donate goods,
services, and forgive myself, Jen, for the way I am built.

On Lion Road

They lie like sliced mushrooms, overgrown portobellos,
brewed coffee backs to crème brûlée bellies, curving in

on themselves, fifteen or more cats crowding the dirt track,
a pride bigger than average, with a handful of adolescent

males not yet run off to start their own teams.
At the moment they're enough to make a play

for hippos, bring down giraffe, and even now
they lick blood from each other's fur, a *lagniappe*

from last night's kill, while shifting at every noise,
some standing to probe further, then settling

again, ears pinned into the wind and the Land Rover's
purr that will travel no further forward.

We are all scarred by lack of sleep.
Who are the kings, who are the men?

As the jeep off-roads into a three-point
turn to head back to the lodge, there is no telling

in the rearview if they lag behind or, as it is written,
they are closer than they appear.

www.ingramcontent.com/pod-product-compliance
Lightning Source LLC
Chambersburg PA
CBHW060508080526
44584CB00015B/1598